Giulia   Silvia

This atlas was developed in collaboration with
researchers from the National Institute for Nuclear Physics in Italy,
curious women and men
trained in the study of the extraordinary phenomena
of the world around us every day.

Look for their faces...
one day you might be one of them!

CONTENTS

A FEW NUMBERS...

Gt = metric gigaton
1 Gt/year corresponds to one billion metric tons per year.

571

plant species extinct in the last 250 years, especially in locations with a tropical or Mediterranean climate.

15
billion

trees that humans cut down each year, replacing them with only 5 billion new plants. Tropical regions suffer the most from deforestation.

467

species declared extinct from 2010 to 2020. There are about one million currently at risk and likely to face the same end.

8
million tons

of **plastic** that end up in the oceans every year, creating serious problems for marine ecosystems.

24
Gt/year

of **fertile soil** lost in the world because of desertification, soil degradation and drought, with dire consequences on the lives of millions of people.

250
Gt/year

of **glacier ice** lost in Greenland from 2000 to 2020. The Arctic is warming much faster than the rest of the planet.

0.8°C
(33°F)

the **increase in the average surface temperature** of the planet (earth and oceanic) in the period between 1880 and 2012.

71%

the earth's surface covered by **water.**

29%

the earth's surface **above water.**

200
Gt/year

of **glacier ice** that has been lost in Antarctica from 2010 to 2020... much more than in previous decades! In the previous decade the loss was equal to 80 Gt/year.

48

species of birds and mammals at risk of extinction saved through human interventions from 1993 to 2020.

A PLANET AT RISK

What environmental problems will we discuss in this book?

GLOBAL WARMING

The increase in the earth's temperature causes glaciers and ice caps to melt. This, in turn, causes the **sea level to rise**, which, over time, causes islands and coastal areas to be submerged, destroying diverse natural habitats, home to many living beings.

DEFORESTATION

Deforestation by humans demolishes **entire forests** in order to obtain timber or land and pastures for cultivation. It has been calculated that around 200,000 km^2 (77,000 sq mi) of tropical forest are lost every year.

POLLUTION

An enormous quantity of substances is introduced by humans into the air, water and soil, with serious effects on the environment, the health of living species and the climate. In this book we will talk about **plastic in the oceans**. In fact, plastic is one of the major polluting materials. The situation is growing dire, especially when we consider the impact this material has on our environment: it damages marine ecosystems and compromises the entire food chain, reaching us.

DESERTIFICATION

Desertification is caused by the intensive exploitation of the land for farming or raising livestock, causing climate change that releases carbon emissions into the atmosphere. This process leads to the **degradation of the soil** and the disappearance of flora and fauna, making the natural environment inhospitable.

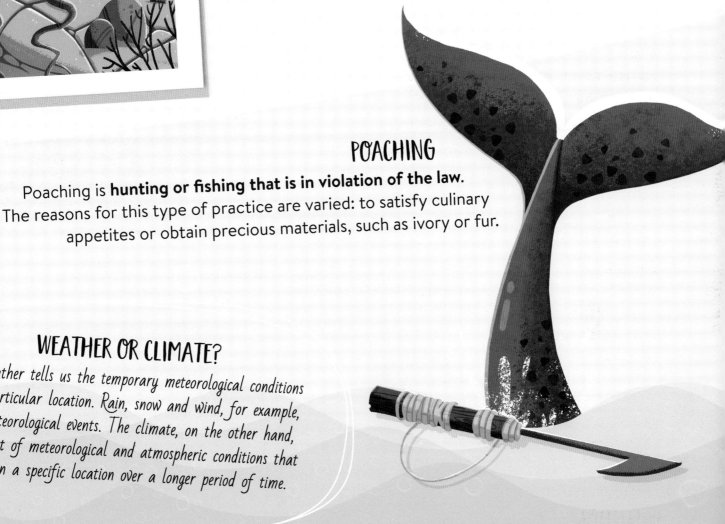

POACHING

Poaching is **hunting or fishing that is in violation of the law.** The reasons for this type of practice are varied: to satisfy culinary appetites or obtain precious materials, such as ivory or fur.

WEATHER OR CLIMATE?

The weather tells us the temporary meteorological conditions at a particular location. Rain, snow and wind, for example, are meteorological events. The climate, on the other hand, is the set of meteorological and atmospheric conditions that occur in a specific location over a longer period of time.

About 8 million tons of waste end up in the oceans every year.

The most common waste in the sea:

Plastic bags   Plastic bottles   Cigarette butts

SPECIES EXTINCT BECAUSE OF HUMANS

Over time the inhabitants of our planet have found ways to adapt to their environment. The spread of humans, however, has caused severe changes to Earth's habitats. Many species have become extinct as a result. Here are a few!

Passenger pigeon
(Ectopistes migratorius)

The passenger pigeon was widespread in **North America**. It became extinct because of the destruction of its colonies by humans, logging and hunting.

Year of last sighting

1878

Antarctic wolf *(Dusicyon australis)*

The Antarctic wolf was the only native land mammal to inhabit the **Falkland Islands**. It was hunted because it was considered a danger to sheep: its extinction was caused precisely by this.

1876

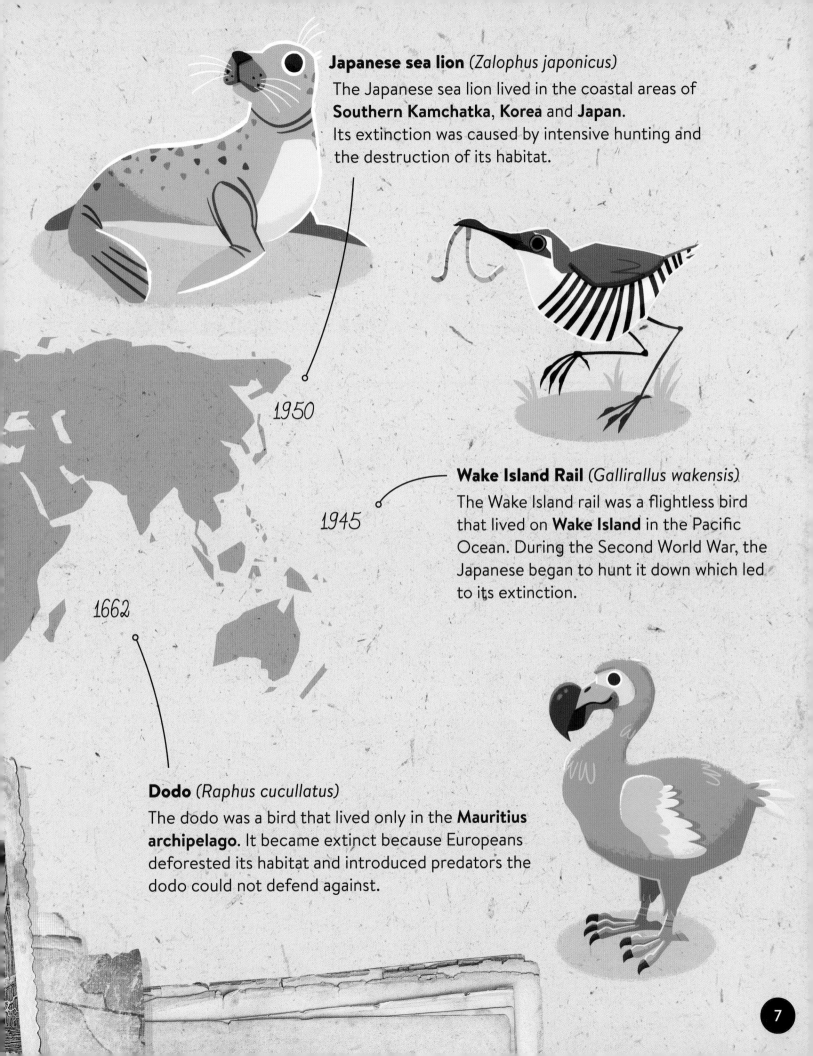

Japanese sea lion (*Zalophus japonicus*)

The Japanese sea lion lived in the coastal areas of **Southern Kamchatka**, **Korea** and **Japan**. Its extinction was caused by intensive hunting and the destruction of its habitat.

1950

1945

1662

Wake Island Rail (*Gallirallus wakensis*)

The Wake Island rail was a flightless bird that lived on **Wake Island** in the Pacific Ocean. During the Second World War, the Japanese began to hunt it down which led to its extinction.

Dodo (*Raphus cucullatus*)

The dodo was a bird that lived only in the **Mauritius archipelago.** It became extinct because Europeans deforested its habitat and introduced predators the dodo could not defend against.

THE POLAR REGIONS

ARCTIC... OR ANTARCTICA?

Located at the **North Pole** is the **Arctic**, an enormous plate of ice surrounded by the sea, cold and desolate, characterized by severe changes in temperature from season to season.

Which of the two poles is colder? You may be amazed to know that the South Pole is colder than the North Pole!

Located at the **South Pole**, on the other hand, is **Antarctica**, a true continent, a land covered by ice surrounded by the ocean. It is the largest concentration of ice on the planet: a reserve of fresh water that is precious to all life!

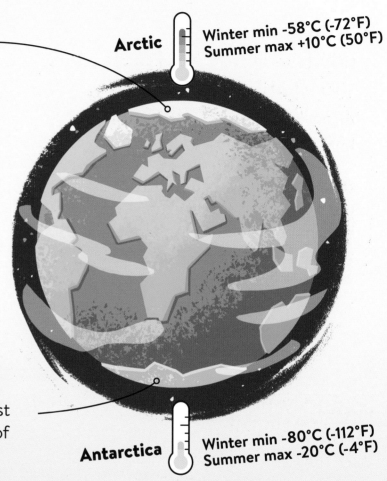

Arctic
Winter min -58°C (-72°F)
Summer max +10°C (50°F)

Antarctica
Winter min -80°C (-112°F)
Summer max -20°C (-4°F)

I live in the North Pole!

Walrus

The poles are covered in perennial ice and snow, and the climatic conditions in these areas are very harsh. However, these regions are changing rapidly because of climate change, and the animals that inhabit them struggle to adapt.

HOW DO ANIMALS AND PLANTS SURVIVE THE POLAR CLIMATE?

All animals and plants that live in the polar regions have had to adapt to low temperatures. Animals generally have **thick fur and layers of fat** to survive the cold. Among these, the polar bear is the most famous, but there are also the reindeer, muskox, ermine, seal, walrus and penguin.

WHAT IS THE ARCTIC HIDING?

The **seeds of thousands of plant species** are stored in an underground storehouse on the Svalbard Islands to preserve and convey them in the event of climate change and famine.

DO YOU KNOW THAT POLAR BEARS DO NOT HAVE WHITE FUR?

Even though they are called white bears, they actually have **transparent fur**: reflecting the light makes the fur look white!

I live in the North and South Pole!

We live at the South Pole!

We live at the North Pole!

Seal

Penguins

Polar bear

DO YOU KNOW...

1 m (3.3 ft)
3 kg (6.6 lb)

The tusks of the **walrus** are very long canines that can reach 1 m (3.3 ft) in length and weigh more than 3 kg (6.6 lb) each!

Orcas live in groups and have a true language: they communicate with each other using sounds!

There are also very small organisms, such as **krill**, an Antarctic crustacean that reaches a maximum of 6 cm (2.4 in) in length and a weight of 2 g (0.07 oz). It is one of the most abundant species on the planet!

2 g (0.07 oz)

ENDANGERED SPECIES

The main enemy of the poles' inhabitants is not so much humans as much as the impact of human activity on the polar territory: **climate change** exposes the inhabitants of the Artic to new, sometimes lethal, challenges.

WHAT IF THE KRILL DISAPPEAR?

These Antarctic crustaceans feed on **algae**. If all the ice melted, the algae would disappear, causing a catastrophe: there would be no more food for the krill and consequently for the fish, seals, penguins and other animals.

Penguins, in the course of evolution, lost the ability to fly, but they are, in fact, birds.

The female of the species of the Adélie penguins lays only one egg in each brood and entrusts it to the male, who incubates it between its webbed feet until the egg is ready to hatch.

The narwhal is called 'unicorn of the sea' thanks to its unmistakable 'tusk' that protrudes from its snout. The tusk is actually a spiral tooth that can grow up to 2.7 m (8.8 ft).

The arctic fox withstands temperatures as low as 50°C below zero (-58°F). Its coat adapts to the environment: in winter it is white or grey-white and in summer it can be white or grey with tones of brown.

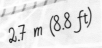

2.7 m (8.8 ft)

HOW WILL NARWHALS BE ABLE TO COMMUNICATE WITH EACH OTHER?

Narwhals communicate through sounds, so are greatly affected by the noise caused by ships. When the ice melts, new navigation paths for ships open and the narwhals find it increasingly difficult to hear each other, to orient themselves and to take care of their children.

WHAT WILL THE ARCTIC FOXES EAT?

Lemmings are the preferred prey of arctic foxes, which hunt them in the snow. Because of rising temperatures, the natural hollows that are created by the snow cover, in which these small rodents live and find food, no longer form.

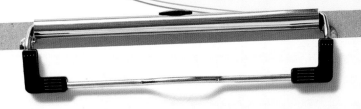

A word from... RESEARCHERS AT WORK

WHAT ARE THE SECRETS HIDDEN IN THE ICE OF THE SOUTH POLE?

Snow, which will become ice, settles on the ground and traps small bubbles of air and dust (**particulates**). So, layer by layer, a sort of encyclopaedia of past climates is formed: analysing the deepest ice allows us to study what the air was like thousands of years ago.

Surface

2,000 years

10,000 years

130,000 years

Ice layers

Ice core

The longest ice core ever extracted measured over 3 km (1.9 mi)! Analysing the deepest section allows us to study what the air was like about 800,000 years ago!

HOW IS THE ICE COLLECTED?

Scientists drill into the ice with large, powerful **drills** and extract ice cylinders called **cores**. Once extracted, an ice core is divided into different portions, which are then studied and stored in laboratory **freezers** around the world.

CAN YOU LIVE IN THE SOUTH POLE?

At the South Pole there are scientific research stations where researchers and people from all over the world live. The **research stations** may be open all year round or only during certain seasons, hosting different numbers of people. These facilities include laboratories, living quarters, food and fuel storage areas, as well as various landing zones.

WHO LIVES AT THESE RESEARCH STATIONS?

In each research station there are scientists: physicists, chemists, biologists and astronomers who make observations and collect samples, and also doctors and all the people who work in the management of the station, such as cooks, electricians, plumbers and mechanics.

WHAT DO THEY DO?

From observations of the ice, atmosphere and marine environment, it is possible to study climate change at a global level. Furthermore, the climatic conditions in Antarctica make it one of the best places in the world for observations of Space.

WHAT IS LIFE LIKE?

Working at a research station is not easy: the climate is extreme, day or night can last for months, and isolation is guaranteed!

ANTARCTICA

30+
nations present

70+
permanent research stations

1,000
winter residents

4,000
summer residents

13

GLOBAL WARMING

Global warming is a climatic phenomenon in which the average temperature on Earth increases.

As if Earth had a fever!

WHAT IS THE GREENHOUSE EFFECT?

The **sun's rays** are in part reflected by the earth, especially by clouds and snow surfaces, and in part absorbed. The earth therefore heats up and, in turn, emits rays of infrared radiation (invisible to the human eye). Instead of returning to Space, these rays may become 'trapped' by certain gases present in the atmosphere, such as carbon dioxide (CO_2). The atmosphere and the greenhouse effect are necessary for life on our planet, because they allow for the reduction of temperature variation and make it less cold.

Transportation

Combustion

Industry

WHY IS THERE GLOBAL WARMING?

In recent decades, however, the greenhouse effect has intensified significantly, according to scientists due to human activities that have generated large additional amounts of greenhouse gases, causing an increase in the average temperature on Earth. Human activities, for example, have increased the amount of carbon dioxide in the atmosphere by more than one-third since the nineteenth century.

WHAT ARE THE CONSEQUENCES?

The increase in Earth's temperature causes the **ice caps and glaciers to melt**, which causes a rise in the sea level. It also causes other significant changes: more extreme weather (hurricanes and storms), the quantity and seasonality of rain, the flowering and growth times of plants (with serious consequences to agriculture) and ocean acidification (damaging coral reefs).

WHERE CAN THESE EFFECTS BE SEEN?

The effects are evident not only in the polar regions but also in other areas of the planet. For example, some areas are becoming **more and more arid**, with possible serious consequences for ecosystems and the people who live there.

WHAT CAN WE DO?

In our own small way, **each of us can do something** to limit the amount of carbon dioxide and other greenhouse gases produced in our daily activities.

For example, choose alternative means of transportation to go to school or to travel with the family: bicycle, public transport or walking.

FORESTS

Forests are Earth's lungs: these environments, in fact, produce oxygen, without which we could not survive. Despite this, most forests are cut down or destroyed, causing gravely serious environmental consequences.

WHAT IS A FOREST?

A forest is a natural area where the earth's surface is covered with **tall trees**.

Attention: sometimes we use the term 'forest' as a synonym for 'woods' and vice versa. Forests, however, are much larger and often older than woods!

HOW MANY KINDS OF FORESTS ARE THERE?

The world's forests are classified according to geographical and botanical criteria.

From a **geographical point of view** there are these types of forests:

- boreal
- temperate
- tropical
- subtropical

From a **botanical point of view** there are these types of forests:

- **coniferous forests**
- **deciduous forests** (which lose their leaves in autumn)
- **sclerophyll forests** (with shrubs and low trees with hard and leathery leaves)
- **tropical forests and rainforests**

HOW DO PLANTS FEED THEMSELVES?

Plants get their food from the sun using a biochemical process called '**photosynthesis**'.

Photosynthesis uses the energy from sunlight exposure to convert carbon dioxide and water into nutrients.

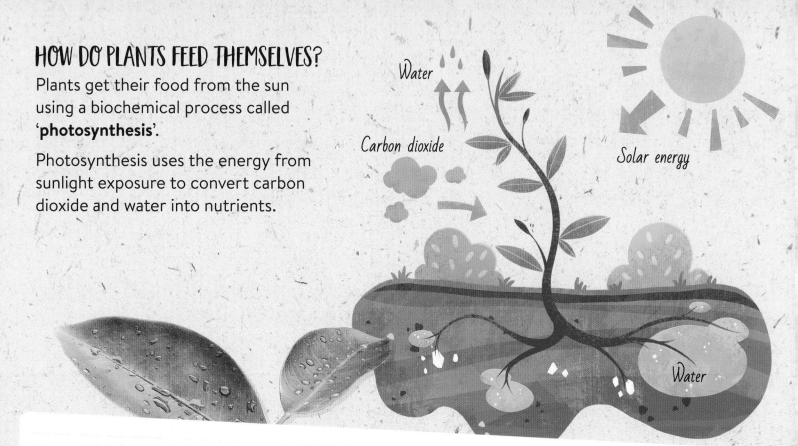

Water

Carbon dioxide

Solar energy

Water

DO YOU KNOW THAT FORESTS HELP TO COMBAT CLIMATE CHANGE?

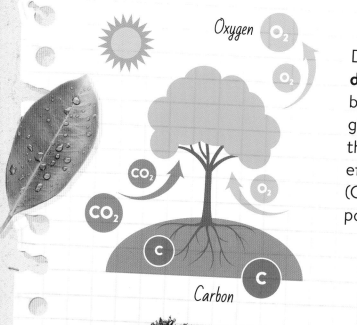

Oxygen

O_2

O_2

CO_2

CO_2

O_2

C

C

Carbon

During photosynthesis, billions of tons of **carbon dioxide** (CO_2) are transformed into **oxygen** (O_2) by plants. In this way, forests can counteract global warming by absorbing part of the CO_2 that causes the increase in the greenhouse effect. In addition, forests, by storing **carbon** (C) in the soil through the plant roots, make life possible for plants and animals.

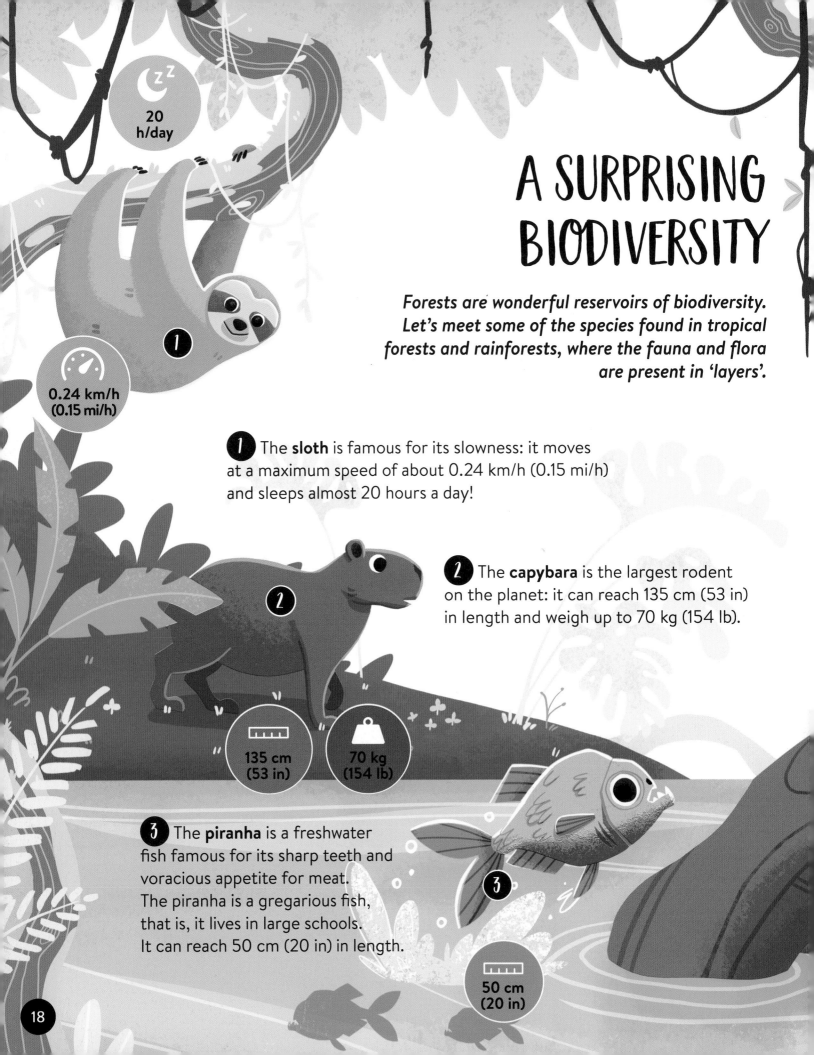

A SURPRISING BIODIVERSITY

Forests are wonderful reservoirs of biodiversity. Let's meet some of the species found in tropical forests and rainforests, where the fauna and flora are present in 'layers'.

20 h/day

0.24 km/h (0.15 mi/h)

1 The **sloth** is famous for its slowness: it moves at a maximum speed of about 0.24 km/h (0.15 mi/h) and sleeps almost 20 hours a day!

2 The **capybara** is the largest rodent on the planet: it can reach 135 cm (53 in) in length and weigh up to 70 kg (154 lb).

135 cm (53 in)

70 kg (154 lb)

3 The **piranha** is a freshwater fish famous for its sharp teeth and voracious appetite for meat. The piranha is a gregarious fish, that is, it lives in large schools. It can reach 50 cm (20 in) in length.

50 cm (20 in)

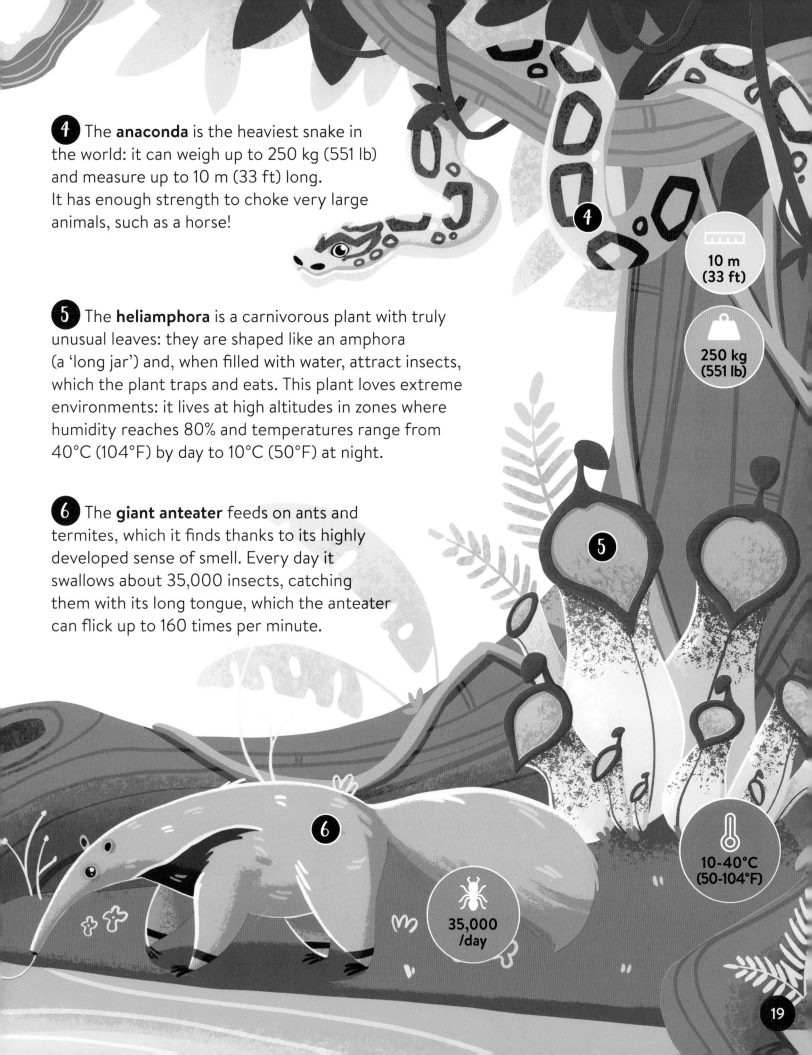

4 The **anaconda** is the heaviest snake in the world: it can weigh up to 250 kg (551 lb) and measure up to 10 m (33 ft) long.
It has enough strength to choke very large animals, such as a horse!

5 The **heliamphora** is a carnivorous plant with truly unusual leaves: they are shaped like an amphora (a 'long jar') and, when filled with water, attract insects, which the plant traps and eats. This plant loves extreme environments: it lives at high altitudes in zones where humidity reaches 80% and temperatures range from 40°C (104°F) by day to 10°C (50°F) at night.

6 The **giant anteater** feeds on ants and termites, which it finds thanks to its highly developed sense of smell. Every day it swallows about 35,000 insects, catching them with its long tongue, which the anteater can flick up to 160 times per minute.

10 m
(33 ft)

250 kg
(551 lb)

10-40°C
(50-104°F)

35,000
/day

19

THREATENED SPECIES

The forest is the home of biodiversity: 80% of land animal species are concentrated within this wonderful habitat.

The **Amur leopard** is found in the temperate forests of Korea, north-eastern China and eastern Russia. It takes its name from the Amur River, one of the longest rivers in the world, located in Eastern Siberia. Unfortunately, today only a few dozen members of this species remain.

In the forests of central Africa, **gorillas** are severely threatened by poaching, disease and deforestation.

The **platypus**, which looks like a cross between a duck and a beaver, is a peculiar mammal because... it lays eggs! Its survival is threatened by frequent Australian droughts, but even more so by the fires that hit Australia in early 2020.

The **Sumatran tiger** is the main forest predator of the island of Sumatra. Because of deforestation and poaching, fewer and fewer members of this species remain.

The **rhinoceros** is at risk of extinction because of its precious horn: poachers hunt the rhinoceros for its horn to sell at exorbitant prices on the black market.

In China, half the forests have been cleared to construct roads and buildings. The **panda** lives in these forests, feeding almost solely on bamboo. However, because of deforestation, this species is in danger of extinction.

The **toucan** is the best-known tropical bird. It is able to adapt to changes affecting its habitat, but the deforestation of the Amazon threatens its existence.

DEFORESTATION

Deforestation, also called 'clearcutting', is the cutting down of entire forests.

Every year humans destroy about 200,000 km² of tropical forest.

WHAT ARE THE MOST AFFECTED AREAS?

One area of the planet most affected by deforestation is the **Amazon**, a vast region of South America. It is a place that offers food and shelter to tens of thousands of animal species, many of which have yet to be discovered.

350
indigenous
communities

25%
of the flora and
fauna of the planet

17-20%
of the world's
water reserves

6.7
million km²
of forest

427
species
of mammals

1,300
species
of birds

3,000
species
of fish

1,200
species
of butterflies

60,000
species
of plants

WHAT ARE THE CAUSES?

Humans cut down forests to acquire **wood**, used in industry and building houses, and to clear land to make new space for the construction of **cities** and **roads** or for **agricultural activities**. In the Amazon rainforest, for example, trees are burned to make space for **raising cattle** and to convert land for agricultural use.

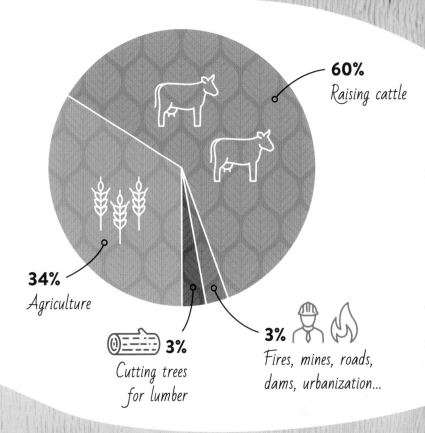

60%
Raising cattle

34%
Agriculture

3%
Cutting trees for lumber

3%
Fires, mines, roads, dams, urbanization...

WHAT DO WE LOSE WITH THE FORESTS?

Forests are indispensable for the planet: they reduce the greenhouse effect, protect the soil, produce food and are home to diverse peoples, such as the **Amazonian Indians**, who, having survived the adversity and conquests of foreign peoples, live still today along the rivers.

WHAT CAN WE DO?

The first thing we can do is avoid supporting companies that do not contribute to the **sustainable development** of our planet.

We can, for example, look for brands that certify a product's origin from **responsibly managed forests**. This book was made using this type of paper!

We can also avoid eating beef from non-sustainable sources.

DESERTS

Deserts are arid and inhospitable areas...they really seem incompatible with life!
On the contrary, the desert is abundant in flora and fauna. The plants and animals
that live here have adapted to the arid climate and little rainfall.

WHAT ARE THE CHARACTERISTICS OF HOT DESERTS?

In hot deserts the temperatures are extreme: reaching **50°C (122°F)** during the day and
dropping close to freezing at night. In addition to extreme temperatures, the animals and
plants that live there must also adapt to **extreme aridity**. Rain is very rare: on average only
a few millimetres per year.

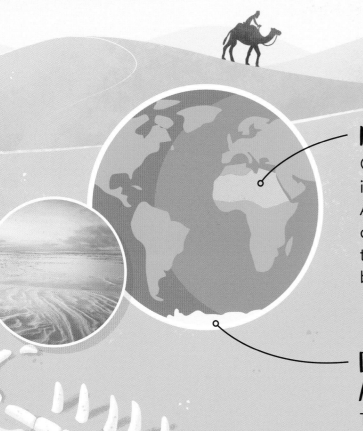

HAVE DESERTS ALWAYS BEEN DESERTS?

One of the deserts you have surely heard of
is the **Sahara**, which is located in Africa.
At one time, this expanse of dunes was
covered with lush vegetation, according to
the data from numerous fossil finds dating
back to the Neolithic Era.

DID YOU KNOW THAT DESERTS ARE NOT ALL HOT?

There are hot deserts and cold deserts.
Antarctica can be considered the largest desert
in the world, despite being completely covered
with ice: its surface area measures as much as
one and a half times that of Europe!

WHAT PLANTS LIVE IN DESERTS? HOW DO THEY SURVIVE?

The most common species in deserts are **succulent plants**, but there are also lichens and cacti. Many plants remain as seeds for years, only to bloom during short periods of rain. Others have very long roots to reach groundwater. Most do not have leaves, but thorns, preventing the loss of water.

© Shutterstock / Yavuz Sariyildiz

DO HUMAN POPULATIONS ALSO LIVE HERE?

Human populations living in deserts have had to adapt their lifestyle to the severe conditions of the environment. The **Tuareg**, for example, a nomadic people who live in the Sahara, raise livestock and practice agriculture only in the oases.

...AND THE ANIMALS?

Most of the animals are active at night.

The **mammals** that live here are desert foxes and dogs, horses, sheep and dromedaries.

There are also **reptiles**, such as snakes, lizards and tortoises, and **amphibians**, such as frogs and toads, which live in burrows to escape the intense heat.

Then there are also various species of necrophagous **birds** (that is, birds that feed on carcasses), such as vultures and crows, as well as species of **insects**, such as locusts and scorpions.

25

DESERT SPECIES

Camels and **dromedaries** are the perfect desert animals. In addition to a reserve of fat in their humps, they have also very long eyelashes, thick hair in the ears and closable nostrils to protect themselves from the sand, as well as flat, cushioned feet for walking easily on the dunes.

Meerkats have a particular black colour around the eyes that absorbs sunlight to prevent it from reflecting into the pupils: in this way they can see clearly during the day.

Road runners eliminate excess salts from their body not through urine but through a gland located right next to their eyes, in order not to waste the precious mineral salts.

The **desert viper** of Namibia uses a very particular method to travel across the burning sand: it moves sideways, or sidewinds, touching the ground only at two points.

If necessary, **scorpions** can slow their metabolism and enter a state of hibernation that can last up to a year. During this period, however, they are able to react to attacks from predators with lightning-fast reflexes.

The **African ground squirrel**, originally from the driest areas of South Africa, uses its thick furry tail to shade and cover itself, just like a tried and true umbrella!

It is not true that no one can get close to cacti because of their thorns! **Peccaries**, mammals related to pigs, have learned to feed on these plants without hurting themselves.

The **thorny devil** has thorns crossed like sorts of 'channels' that bring the little water available directly to the lizard's mouth.

Fennecs, small foxes of the North African desert, have very large ears. These allow them both to perceive the vibrations of prey hidden in the sand and to disperse the heat through their blood vessels.

DESERT PLANTS

There are different types of **palm**: the most prized is the date palm, its fruit a main source of energy for human desert inhabitants, along with dromedary milk and meat from the cattle they raise. Date palms can reach 10 m (33 ft) high, and *legmi*, a sugary nectar, is made from the fermented sap of the tree.

10 m (33 ft)

The **saguaro** is a tree-like cactus that lives in Arizona. Its growth is very slow, and it can take up to 75 years before its characteristic branches are formed. Its structure allows it to store a huge amount of water, up to 5 tons. Its longevity is also incredible: the saguaro can live up to 300 years.

5 t

300 years

3.5 m (11.5 ft)

25 cm (10 in)

150 years

The **barrel cactus** is one of the largest specimens of the American southwestern deserts: it measures up to 3.5 m (11.5 ft) high, and its thorns can reach 25 cm (10 in). It can live up to 150 years and withstand 6 years without water.

28

The **tamarind** has edible fruits, widely used in Middle Eastern and African cuisine. This tree can reach 30 m (98 ft) high, and it can become completely submerged in sand. Once dead, the tree provides much wood for the desert nomadic tribes.

30 m (98 ft)

The **salsola** has developed the most effective strategies to survive and reproduce. The deep roots allow it to find water everywhere and to become a round and vaporous bush. In the fall, the stem breaks off at the base and the plant begins to roll and travel across plains, fields and roads, commonly known as 'tumbleweed'.

The **desert gourd** belongs to the same family as pumpkins, squash, and watermelons, but its fruit is not edible to humans. The dromedaries, however, find it delicious!

DESERTIFICATION

WHAT IS DESERTIFICATION?

Intensive land use and **climate change** cause desertification: flora and fauna disappear and soils degrade, turning the natural environment inhospitable to the most common forms of life.

WHAT CAN WE DO TO COMBAT DESERTIFICATION?

Many countries are thinking about the reforestation of desert areas.

One of the best-known examples is the **Great Green Wall**: a project to create a real forest wall that crosses the width of Africa. Other states are investing in restoring degraded areas, creating new legislation focused on the protection and sustainable use of land.

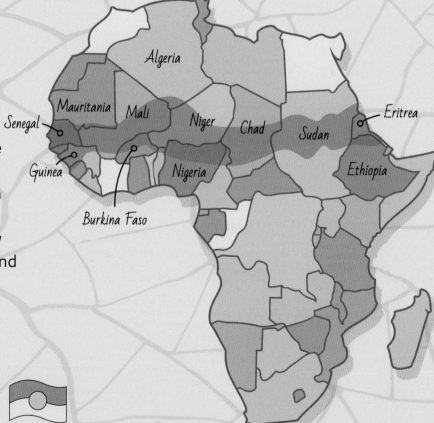

7,600 km
long

15 km
wide

20+
countries involved

Some of the participating countries

CAUSED BY NATURE OR THE FAULT OF HUMANS?

In some areas, desertification can be influenced mainly by climatic factors; in others, especially the mild zones, this process is caused mainly by the actions of humans.

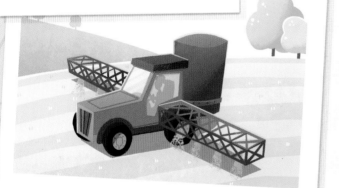

Intensive agriculture

The improper use of agricultural machinery and industrial fertilizers and the failure to alternate the type of cultivation cause an impoverishment of the land.

Deforestation

The indiscriminate felling of the forest mantle, which increases the exposure of soil to degradation, is one of the main causes of desertification.

Incorrect irrigation

Irrigating with water high in mineral salts deposits a saline layer onto the soil, which increases over time and makes the soil less and less fertile.

Excessive grazing

When cattle are grazed without adequate rest intervals for the land, the soil erodes, triggering desertification.

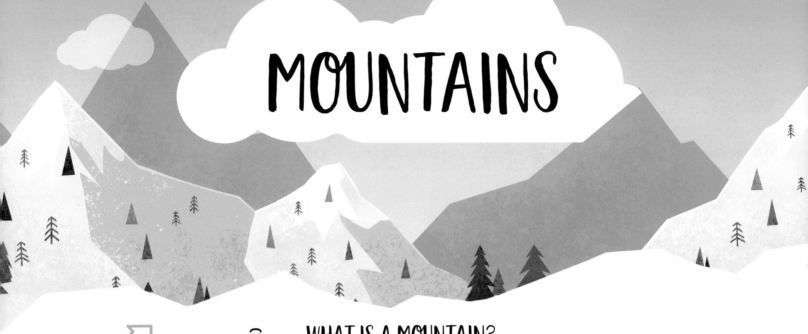

MOUNTAINS

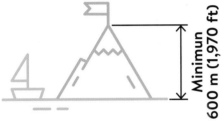

Minimun 600 m (1,970 ft)

WHAT IS A MOUNTAIN?

A mountain is raised ground that has a height of more than 600 m (1,970 ft) above sea level. The height of a mountain is known as its **altitude** and is measured with an altimeter. The starting point for measuring is sea level.

HOW WERE THE MOUNTAINS FORMED?

Some mountains formed from the **currugation** of the earth's crust, when, in the past, the ground rose from the collision of the tectonic plates. Others were created by **magma**, the incandescent lava formed from the melting of rocks and their solidification in contact with air, emerging from the earth's crust.

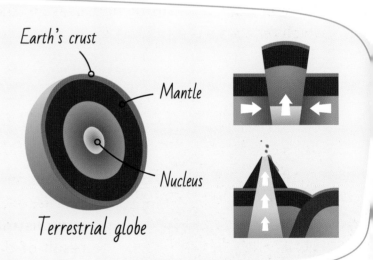

Earth's crust

Mantle

Nucleus

Terrestrial globe

ARE VOLCANOS MOUNTAINS?

Volcanos are particular mountains: the result of different lava flows that have solidified over time but have not 'closed'. The **chimney**, in fact, remains open and more lava periodically emerges from the crater to further change the volcano's appearance. All over the world there are volcanos that are 'extinct' and volcanos that are still active.

The mountains are the highest places on the planet. For a long time they remained unexplored, but today humans have reached their highest peaks. Climate change also affects these colossal peaks, making them vulnerable environments.

WHAT IS THE HIGHEST MOUNTAIN IN THE WORLD?

At 8,848 m (29,031 ft), **Everest** is the highest mountain on the planet. Its record, however, is valid only if the height is measured from sea level: if instead we measure from the centre of the earth, due to the swelling of the globe near the equator the tallest mountain would be **Chimborazo**, one of the highest peaks of the Andes, which reaches 6,310 m (20,548 ft) above sea level.

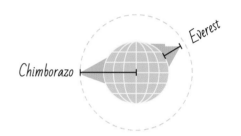

WHY DO WE FIND FOSSILS OF MARINE ANIMALS ON THE MOUNTAINS?

On the mountains it is possible to find many **fossils**, even of marine life, such as fish and shells, demonstrating that mountains were formed as a result of the raising of the seabed.

What does the shape of a mountain tell us?
The peaks of the older mountains, due to erosion, tend to appear smoother, while those of the younger mountains are more rugged and pointed.

MOUNTAIN ANIMALS

1 The **squirrel** lives up to an altitude of 1,000 (3,280 ft); it can have fur that is brown, with small reddish tones, or grey. Squirrels often forget where they bury acorns: because of this, many trees are born every year thanks to them.

2 The **brown bear** is one of the largest land mammals in Europe and its coat is brown. It is not a social animal and leads a solitary life. It is shy with its fellow bears and with other species, especially with humans.

3 The **robin** is a bird of inexhaustible vivacity. During the breeding season, these birds mark the boundary of their territory by singing, and intimidate rivals by displaying their distinctive orange chest.

4 After moulting, the fur of the **ermine** turns completely white, which allows it to blend in with the snowy landscape. It takes refuge mainly in rodent burrows, in wood piles and among stones.

5 The eyes of the **owl** are fixed in their sockets, so they cannot rotate. On the other hand, the owl's head can turn up to 270 degrees, or 135 degrees to each side. To look around, the owl therefore moves its head, and can even see...directly behind itself!

6 The agility of the **chamois** in moving between rocks and on rough terrain is mainly because of the structure of its hooves, with a flexible sole and thin, hard edge. Its habitat includes rocky areas and alpine pastures, mainly between 1,500 and 2,500 m (4,920-8,200 ft) above sea level.

7 The **marmot** lives in the Alps and in the Carpathians. It has a large head, with eyes positioned to give it a broad field of vision. It has developed incisors and a furry tail with a black tuft at the end.

8 The **wolf** is a canid found in remote areas of North America and Eurasia. Wolves live in packs and their social structure is greatly hierarchical: the pack leader is the alpha male, immediately followed by its partner.

ALPINE STRATA

FLORA

ABOVE 3,000 METRES (9,840 FEET):
mosses, lichens and some low-lying, hardy plants, such as edelweiss.

2,000-3,000 METRES (6,600-9,800 FEET):
grassy meadows and bushes.

1,000-2,000 METRES (3,300-6,600 FEET):
coniferous forests,
with fir, pine and larch.

**600-1,000 METRES
(2,000-3,300 FEET):**
large deciduous forests.

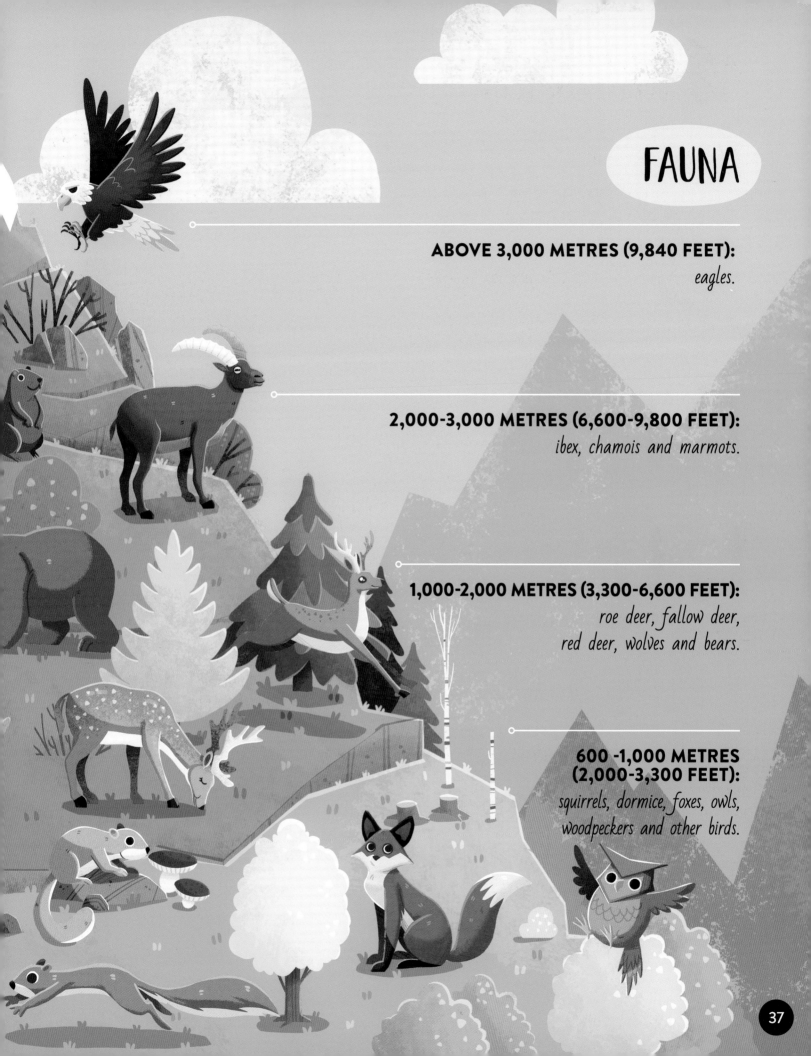

FAUNA

ABOVE 3,000 METRES (9,840 FEET):
eagles.

2,000-3,000 METRES (6,600-9,800 FEET):
ibex, chamois and marmots.

1,000-2,000 METRES (3,300-6,600 FEET):
*roe deer, fallow deer,
red deer, wolves and bears.*

**600 -1,000 METRES
(2,000-3,300 FEET):**
*squirrels, dormice, foxes, owls,
woodpeckers and other birds.*

GLACIERS AT RISK

Mountain glaciers are melting because of rising temperatures, reducing fresh water reserves. Added to this are the effects of anthropization, deforestation and excessive use of water resources.

WHY ARE MOUNTAINS SO IMPORTANT TO US?

Mountain glaciers represent an enormous **reservoir of water** that feeds rivers and streams throughout the year. Humans depend on these reserves: the reduction of these affects the ability to irrigate crops and the availability of drinking water.

WHAT HAPPENS IF THE PERMAFROST MELTS?

With increasing temperatures, **permafrost**, a substrate made up of soil, rock and debris frozen for more than two consecutive years, also melts.

Permafrost is found in the polar regions but is also present in higher mountains, such as the Alps. As permafrost melts, the substrate held together by the ice loses stability and crumbles. If we do nothing to counter the melting of glaciers, floods and erosion will increase, and avalanches could become more frequent, also because of deforestation and intensive agricultural techniques.

Avalanches

Landslides

Floods

WHAT WILL HAPPEN TO THE FAUNA AND FLORA?

The mountainous landscape changes with altitude: as you climb, animals and plants become increasingly scarce. Some species have adapted well to the environment, but if this were destroyed, we could lose truly unique animals and plants.

WHAT NEEDS TO BE DONE TO PREVENT GLACIERS FROM MELTING?

Countries must commit to reducing **CO$_2$ emissions** and neutralizing their impact on the planet, for example by planting more trees and reducing polluting means of transportation, replacing these with efficient and sustainable public transportation.

AND IN OUR OWN SMALL WAY?

To see improvement, we should be inspired by the **mountain people**, who have always lived in harmony with the environment, without altering its balance. We could, for example, eat only fruits and vegetables that are in season or avoid using transportation for a short journey, rather, take a walk in the open air.

PRAIRIES

Prairies are vast expanses where herbaceous and low-lying plants grow, and have been the undisputed kingdom of large herbivores for millennia. Prairies have hot, dry summers and cold, rainy winters. The lack of trees is due not only to climatic factors but also to the grazing of large herbivores from intensive farming.

WHERE ARE PRAIRIES FOUND?

Prairies are widespread on all continents, but they take different names depending on their location: in North America they are called **prairies**, in Asia **steppes**, in Africa **savannas**, in Australia **veld** and in South America **pampas**.

Prairies

Steppes

Savannas

Pampas

Veld

DID YOU KNOW THAT PRAIRIES ARE 'HIGH TRAFFIC' AREAS?

In the savanna, for example, there are many herbivores of considerable size, such as the gnu, zebra, antelope, giraffe, rhinoceros and elephant. Each year, during the **dry season**, herds migrate hundreds of kilometres to reach wetter areas.

Steppe vegetation has always allowed the grazing of large herbivores. It is here that humans, ever since they were nomads, have tamed the horse, establishing a close relationship with this special animal.

AGRICULTURE WAS BORN HERE, TOO!

Seven thousand years ago, in the steppe extending between Anatolia, Mesopotamia and the lower course of the Indus, the oldest urban settlements in the West arose and agriculture developed: wheat, barley and various legumes, such as beans and lentils, were 'domesticated' in these places.

HOW ARE PRAIRIES FORMED?

Prairies are distinguished as natural, semi-natural and cultivated.

Natural prairies
are created naturally,
by a climate of annual rainfall
and seasonal droughts.

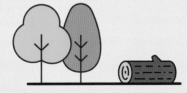

Semi-natural prairies
are the result of
deforestation.

Cultivated prairies,
such as hay fields and
pastures, are made
by humans.

PRAIRIE ANIMALS

1 The **coyote**, also called the prairie wolf, is typical of America and lives in areas between Canada and Colombia. Although it has a solitary temperament, the coyote sometimes gathers in packs. It is easier to hear it than to see it: its high-pitched howl is quite distinct.

2 The **Bolivian vizcacha** is a rodent that can measure up to 60 cm (24 in) in length. Its legs are short but equipped with strong nails that allow it to dig into the ground to build a den. It can weigh about 5 kg (11 lb) and its tail comes off easily, like a lizard's tail, allowing it to escape from traps.

3 The **rhea** is one of the largest birds in the world and is closely related to the ostrich; but while the ostrich lives in Africa, the rhea lives in South America. It cannot fly, but it can run at great speeds thanks to its long and powerful legs.

4 The **armadillo** has a carapace that covers its body and head: this type of 'armour' acts as a protection against possible predators. It lives underground in holes dug by its long and sturdy claws, where it sleeps up to 16 hours a day!

5 The **chimango** is a small bird well known in the prairies of South America, particularly in Argentina, Uruguay and Chile. It feeds on carrion and bones.

6 The **bison** is perhaps the most well-known herbivore of the steppe. Until the last century there were two species: European and North American. Today the European bison is almost extinct, decimated by hunting and the disappearance of its habitat.

7 The **yak** is the symbolic animal of the Tibetan plateau, where it lives among high altitude plains and steppes. It feeds on herbs and herbaceous plants, and sometimes on mosses and lichens. Its habitat can also vary according to the seasons: in cold periods, when food is scarce, some herds undertake great migrations.

8 The **prairie dog** owes its name to its distinct cry, similar to a dog's bark, which it emits to warn its fellow prairie dogs of impending danger. It lives mainly in the western states of the United States and in some areas of Canada and Mexico. Its den is made up of an intricate system of tunnels and galleries that connect several underground chambers.

43

VEGETATION

IS THE PRAIRIE FERTILE GROUND?

Yes, especially in areas where it rains the most during the year. Curiously, the different rodent species that live in the prairie contribute to its fertility. The rodents' **work of digging** mixes, drains and aerates the soil, essential for a prairie's fertility.

ARE THERE TREES IN THE PRAIRIES?

The steppe is commonly made up of grasses and a few kinds of shrubs. Because of the great **changes in temperature**, the rare trees that grow on the prairie survive only near rivers and lakes.

WHY DO ONLY HERBACEOUS PLANTS GROW?

Natural fires and grazing by cattle or wild animals are frequent on the prairies: these factors mean that mostly **grasses** will grow, because grasses regrow much more quickly than woody plants.

WHAT PLANTS ARE FOUND IN THE PRAIRIES?

Grasses, **legumes** and other herbaceous plants bloom from spring to autumn. In the American prairies, for example, pasqueflower and goldenrod grow. In the Russian steppes, on the other hand, irises colour the vast expanses of grass in purple.

Pasqueflower

Iris

Goldenrod

PLANTS = INSECTS = PLANTS

The abundant production of **pollen** by many herbaceous plants is one of the major sources of nourishment for many insects. The insects, in turn, allow pollination and therefore the birth of other plants.

DID YOU KNOW THAT NATURAL FIRES CAN HELP PRAIRIES TO REGENERATE?

During the dry period, fires very often break out. The subsequent rains cause the **mineral nutrients** of the charred remains of plants to penetrate the soil. Immediately after, there is an explosion of green!

45

HUNTING AND POACHING

WHAT IS POACHING?

Poaching is hunting or fishing in **violation of the laws and regulations**.

WHO IS A POACHER?

A poacher is someone who kills protected species, who hunts during prohibited times or in prohibited areas or with prohibited methods and means, or who illegally captures animals. Unfortunately, the practice of poaching happens across all continents.

The **saiga antelope** is a mammal found today only in Russia and Kazakhstan. It became extinct in Romania and Moldova because of unscrupulous hunting in the past. In China, this animal has almost completely disappeared because of poaching: its horn, in fact, is used in traditional Chinese medicine.

In the African savanna the **black rhinoceros** is hunted for its horn, believed to have healing powers. This is why poachers can sell it for large sums of money! Efforts are being made to protect these animals within nature reserves and parks.

The illegal hunting of animals by humans is one of the main causes of damage to the prairie. Here, in fact, numerous species attract poachers, such as the elephant, now at risk of extinction, highly sought for its ivory tusks.

WHY DOES POACHING EXIST?

The reasons are very varied: sometimes it is for reasons of food and others for precious materials, such as ivory or fur.

HOW DO YOU COMBAT IT?

Much has been done and several attempts have been made to resolve the serious situation caused by poaching. Numerous associations are active in different countries, especially environmental protection organizations, engaged in the fight against poaching.

The **pangolin** is a small insectivorous mammal. It lives in Asia and Africa, and is at risk of extinction mainly because of illegal hunting. The Chinese pangolin, in particular, is highly coveted by poachers for its scales.

Przewalski's horse is a very ancient and now very rare Mongolian herbivore, with only 200 members of the species left in the world today. It was the victim of poachers who hunted it for its meat. Today it is slowly repopulating the steppes and prairies where it had once been hunted.

OCEANS AND SEAS

SEA OR OCEAN?

Both are expanses of saltwater, but oceans are much broader and deeper, with only the continents as their borders. Seas, on the other hand, are less vast with shallower depths.

HOW DO WAVES FORM?

Waves are formed by the **wind**! The wind blows on the surface of the sea, pushing the water with a movement that creates **ripples**, which follow each other in succession, the water flowing back and forth like a swing. **Sea currents** also help create waves.

Wind

Length

Height

Crest

Barrel

Sea current

Shoreline

AT THE BOTTOM OF THE SEA... WHAT'S THERE?

The ocean floor is not flat but has steep slopes which, in the deepest spots, are called **trenches** (or **abysses**). They can measure more than 10,000 m (33,000 ft) deep! The record is held by the Mariana Trench in the Pacific Ocean, which is more than 11,000 m (36,000 ft) deep.

The Mariana Trench

48

Our planet is covered by about 71% water. Water is a precious resource that must be protected from possible threats, because it is indispensable for sustaining all forms of life, their survival and evolution.

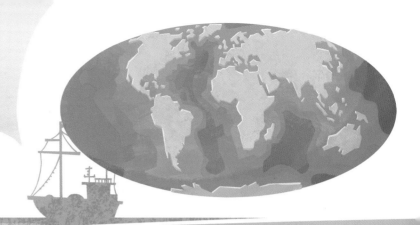

1 litre

35 grams

HOW MUCH SALT IS THERE IN SEAWATER?

On average, a single litre of seawater contains about 35 grams of salt. Considering the earth's oceans and seas contain about 1,380 million cubic kilometres of water (equal to 1,380 billion billion litres), the result is 48.3 million billion tons of salt!

WHY IS THERE SALT IN THE SEA?

Originally, ocean water was not salty: it became so when soluble minerals present in the rocks of the earth's crust began to dissolve. The most abundant mineral salt is **sodium chloride**, our common kitchen salt.

CORAL REEFS

Coral reefs are incredible living organisms composed of corals and madrepores, tiny marine invertebrates similar in shape to that of the octopus, which take thousands of years to grow, reaching truly unimaginable lengths and heights.

WHERE DO CORAL REEFS GROW?

They are found where the water is clear, a little salty and well illuminated, in temperatures between 20 and 30°C (68-86°F). Growing between 40 and 60 m (130-200 ft) deep and needing lots of light, corals grow only in areas with a lot of light. In some areas of the earth, however, there are special coral reefs that exist at lower temperatures and greater depths.

**20-30°C
68-86°F**

**40-60 m
(130-200 ft)**

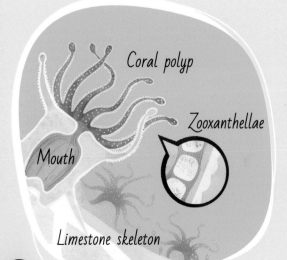

Coral polyp

Zooxanthellae

Mouth

Limestone skeleton

HOW DO THEY FORM?

Corals are created by the work of **coral polyps**, which live in groups and in symbiosis with unicellular algae: the **zooxanthellae**. These provide oxygen, help remove waste and allow the formation of insoluble, rock-hard limestone.

WHAT ARE THE NATURAL THREATS?

Low tides, **earthquakes**, **hurricanes** and **cyclones**. When the water level drops during low tide, coral is exposed to sunlight and heat and risks drying out. Hurricanes, cyclones and earthquakes, on the other hand, damage these creatures with their destructive force. Thankfully though, healthy coral can easily recover from natural disasters!

Hurricane

WHAT ARE THE CONSEQUENCES OF HUMAN ACTIVITY?

Pollution, affecting climate change, causes the water to warm up and also become more acidic. Consequently, the algae that inhabit the coral no longer photosynthesize, causing the coral to bleach. **Wild logging** is also very dangerous, because tree roots no longer hold the debris carried by the torrential rains, which then reaches the sea and suffocates the corals.

And these are just some of the consequences of human action!

CAN ANYTHING BE DONE TO SAFEGUARD CORAL REEFS?

The first thing to do is reduce pollution. Scholars are also recreating **artificial coral reefs** to generate a habitat where the species of this ecosystem can live. Furthermore, some researchers are trying to feed corals artificially.

ANIMALS OF THE CORAL REEF

One-fourth of Earth's marine fauna lives in coral reefs.

1 The **royal gramma**, also known as the 'fairy basslet', lives in the coral reefs of the Caribbean. It has beautiful yellow and purple colours, which appear darker underwater allowing it to blend in.

2 The **porcelain crab**, with a porcelain-coloured body covered in spots, lives under the protection of anemones. It has big claws that it uses to chase away any clownfish who try to steal its home!

3 The **harlequin shrimp**'s name comes from its pearly white colour punctuated by large pink, purple, red and blue spots. It feeds almost exclusively on starfish.

4 The **clownfish** lives in symbiosis with the anemones; its body is covered with a mucus that allows it to defend itself from their sting. Hidden among the tentacles of the anemones, the clownfish protects itself from predators! To return the favour, it brings food it catches to its host.

Maximum size: 5 cm (2 in)

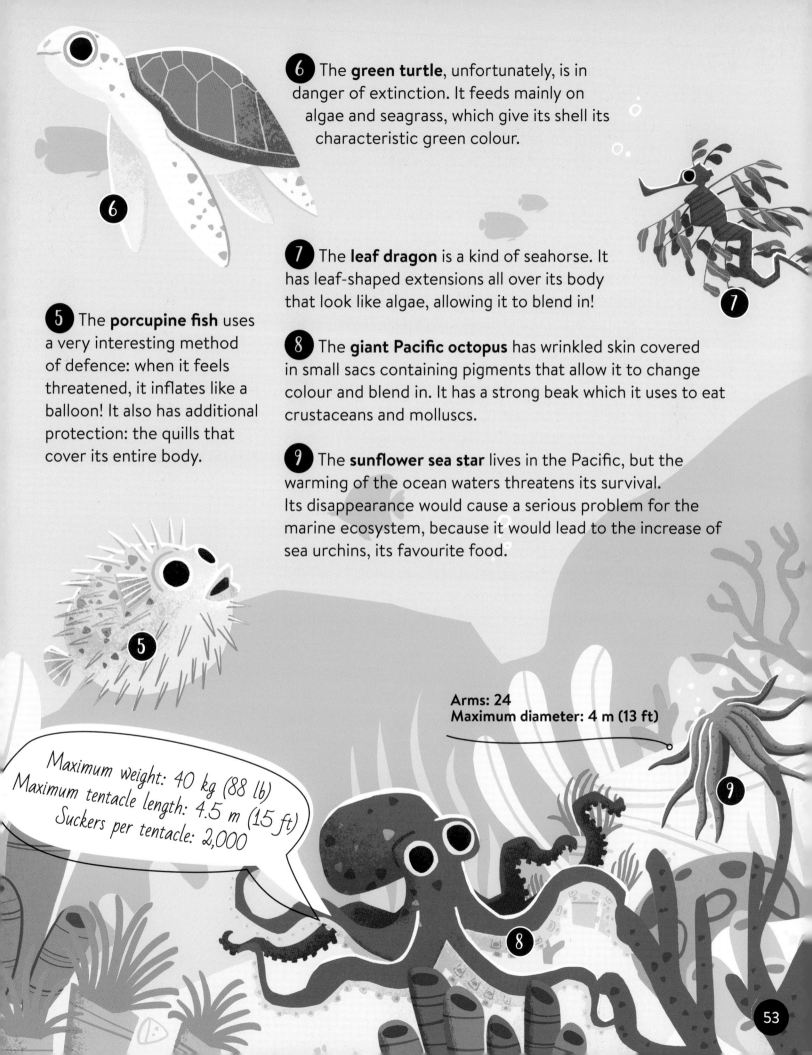

6 The **green turtle**, unfortunately, is in danger of extinction. It feeds mainly on algae and seagrass, which give its shell its characteristic green colour.

7 The **leaf dragon** is a kind of seahorse. It has leaf-shaped extensions all over its body that look like algae, allowing it to blend in!

8 The **giant Pacific octopus** has wrinkled skin covered in small sacs containing pigments that allow it to change colour and blend in. It has a strong beak which it uses to eat crustaceans and molluscs.

9 The **sunflower sea star** lives in the Pacific, but the warming of the ocean waters threatens its survival. Its disappearance would cause a serious problem for the marine ecosystem, because it would lead to the increase of sea urchins, its favourite food.

5 The **porcupine fish** uses a very interesting method of defence: when it feels threatened, it inflates like a balloon! It also has additional protection: the quills that cover its entire body.

Arms: 24
Maximum diameter: 4 m (13 ft)

Maximum weight: 40 kg (88 lb)
Maximum tentacle length: 4.5 m (15 ft)
Suckers per tentacle: 2,000

WATER POLLUTION

Many substances, solid or liquid, can pollute water. Among these is plastic, one of the most popular materials in the world. However, plastic is not easy to recycle: it often ends up in the oceans and seas, endangering not only the health of marine life but also human health.

HOW MUCH PLASTIC IS POLLUTING THE SEA?

Estimates range at 5,300 billion pieces of plastic floating or deposited on the seabed, equal to about 150 million tons.

WHICH OCEAN HAS THE HIGHEST CONCENTRATION OF PLASTIC?

The record for the 'most polluted ocean' belongs to the **Pacific**, with 2,481 billion pieces of plastic debris (equal to 117,420 tons).

About

5,300

billion pieces

1,270
billion pieces

247
billion pieces

1,300
billion pieces

2,481
billion pieces

in the Atlantic Ocean

in the Mediterranean Sea

in the Indian Ocean

in the Pacific Ocean

WHAT WASTE POLLUTES THE WATERS?

The most common waste is: food wrappers, bottle caps, straws, shopping bags, bottles and cigarette butts. Five of these six types of waste are plastic.

WHAT ARE THE CONSEQUENCES?

Plastic has a dramatic impact, both on people's health and on life in our seas: it disintegrates into microplastics, now widespread everywhere, even in the human body. Fish, turtles, dolphins, whales and seabirds ingest it or become trapped, injured and killed.

WHAT CAN WE DO?

We need to try to limit the use of plastic materials. First of all, stop the use of disposable plastic, **plastic that is used only once** and requires very long disposal times. There are many eco-sustainable alternatives, small steps that can make a difference!

LET'S EXPERIMENT!

For all activities, ask for help from an adult!

Are you ready to get your hands 'dirty' with all the interesting facts you have learned so far?

AIR POLLUTION

The air we breathe contains gas, but also small solid particles: 'atmospheric particulate matter'. These particles are in part natural (soil dust, plant debris...), but, especially in cities, many are caused by pollution and are so small that they are not visible to the naked eye. This experiment will help you better understand.

You will need:

A piece of clear plastic · A rectangular stone · Glue · Vaseline · A blank sheet of paper

1 Spread the Vaseline on one surface of the clear plastic, and attach the other surface to the stone with glue.

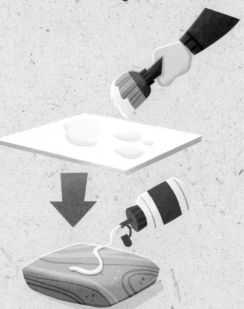

2 Take a photo of the plastic and then leave it outside in a protected place for 24 hours. When the time is up, take the plastic and place it on the sheet of paper: you will be able to see all the particles the Vaseline captured!

What you find trapped is the largest and most macroscopic part of the particles dispersed in the air. There are, however, many other, even smaller particles, which are the main culprits of pollution and may be dangerous to your health when inhaled

COMPOST

In order not to waste organic refuse, you can create compost, which you can then use to fertilize your plants or flowers at home. This experiment will help you understand the process of decomposition of organic waste, which leads to the production of compost.

You will need:

Scissors

An empty two-litre plastic bottle

Potting soil

Leaves, grass and compostable kitchen scraps

Water

1 Remove any label from the bottle and cut off the top. Put a layer of potting soil on the bottom and then cover it with a layer of compostable material. Alternate the layers until the bottle is full.

2 Add a little water to make everything moist, but be careful not to add too much: a puddle should not form on the surface. Then place the bottle outside in a sunny spot. Leave it there for several weeks, and watch the decomposition process!

Leave it there for several weeks, and watch the decomposition process!

THE MELTING OF THE GLACIERS

This experiment will help you understand how glaciers form and melt, and also how they incorporate the dirt and pollutants they find in the course of their life.

You will need:

A small plastic container (without a lid)

A container large enough to hold the small container

Small leaves and debris from the garden

1 Fill the small container with water and place it in the freezer until it freezes.

2 Fill the large container with leaves and other debris you find in the garden. Place it in a sunny area, on a slight slope.

3 Remove the smaller container from the freezer and put it in the large one. Let the ice melt so that the water drips onto the debris.

4 When the ice has melted from the sun's heat, remove the small container and place the large one in the freezer.

Did you notice how the ice changed when it melted and then froze again? And how the dirt was incorporated inside?

OIL

This experiment will help you understand how difficult it is for rescuers to remove oil, perhaps spilled into the sea by a sinking oil tanker, from bird feathers. In fact, oil, like the oil used in this experiment, is not soluble in water; therefore, to clean the birds' wings, water is not enough!

You will need:

A tall glass   Kitchen oil   Food colouring   Dishwashing liquid   A spoon

1 Fill the glass with water. Cover the entire surface of the water with cooking oil. Because water is denser than oil, you will see that the two liquids stay separate, with the oil remaining on top.

2 Add a few drops of food colouring. You will notice these drops do not penetrate the barrier created by the oil; the water remains transparent!

3 Now add two tablespoons of the dish soap, which works as an emulsifier. Did you notice how the soap 'broke through' the layer of oil and the dye was then able to mix with the water?

To remove the oil from birds' wings, therefore, an emulsifying agent is required!

BATTLE OF THE SEED BALLS!

To make the world greener, have fun making these
explosive seed balls, a great way to grow wild flowers!

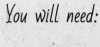

You will need:

A bowl

15 g (0.5 oz)
of wildflower seeds

100 g (3.5 oz)
of dry potting soil

40 g (1.4 oz)
of dry clay (preferably red cerami

1 In the bowl, mix the seeds with the
potting soil. Then add the dry clay and
mix again.

2 Add water a little at a time, continuing to
mix until uniform and you are able to form
balls with a diameter of 2 cm (0.8 in) that
remain intact.

Water

A baking tray

Baking paper

3 Place the balls on the baking tray, arranging them on the baking paper. Let them dry in the sun for a day.

4 Then have fun with the balls throwing them on a dirt ground or in your yard with your friends, and watch them explode!

Thanks to the sun, rain and water you give them, the seeds have everything they need to grow!

CREATE YOUR OWN TERRARIUM!

The terrarium has its own particular micro-climate: sunlight enters through the glass and heats the soil, plants and air in the same way sunlight heats the earth when it enters the atmosphere! Build your own terrarium by following these simple steps.

You will need:

A transparent glass container *

Small plants of different colours and shapes **

Activated charcoal

Sterile soil

Gravel

Small pine cones, shells, miniature animals (optional)

Moss (optional)

Decorative rocks and pebbles (optional)

* You can choose an open or closed container depending on the type of plants you want to use: an aquarium, a goldfish bowl, a cookie container. If, for example, you want to grow succulents, it is better to use an open container, because these plants like a lot of air. If you prefer to plant ferns or ivy, it is better to use a closed container, because these plants love humidity. If you see there is too much condensation on the stopper, however, remove it for a time and then put it back on.

** Try to choose plants all of the same species and above all those that do not get too big in relation to the container.

1. At the bottom of the container, create a layer of gravel about 3 cm (1.2 in) high. Then add a layer of about 1 cm (0.4 in) of activated charcoal: this helps to filter the water and prevent fungi from growing. Finally, fill the container halfway with soil.

2. Plant the plants. When you take them out of their original container, be sure to take the roots as well but remove some of the old soil to help the plants adapt better to the soil of the terrarium. If you use several plants in a large container, arrange them well and a little distant from each other, so they have space to grow.

3. Then you can add moss and decorations as you like.

4. Place the terrarium somewhere out of direct sunlight. Water the plants a little, but be careful not to overwater!

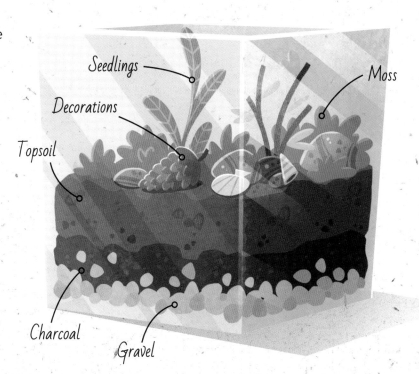

Seedlings

Moss

Decorations

Topsoil

Charcoal

Gravel

Istituto Nazionale di Fisica Nucleare

The INFN, National Institute for Nuclear Physics, is a research institution in Italy that studies the interactions of the elementary components of matter. Scientists discovered that it is precisely by studying the behaviour of infinitely small elements that we can understand the processes that happen in our Universe.

More than 5,000 people are involved in these studies, and recently some have also contributed to two Nobel-prize discoveries: the Higgs boson and gravitational waves. This type of research requires the continuous development of cutting-edge technologies, conceived and implemented at the INFN laboratories, also in collaboration with industry, which often has important consequences to society.

The research is complex and requires collaboration with colleagues from all over the world. Many work outside of Italy at international laboratories, first among them the CERN in Geneva, the European centre dedicated to this research and one of the largest laboratories in the world.

INFN scientists, therefore, have the duty, and also the pleasure, of sharing their work and the results with society, discussing their research and its consequences on everyone's life, including yours.

This book was created through collaboration with:

GIULIA CALZOLAI

A researcher at the INFN, Giulia Calzolai as a child was undecided whether to be an archaeologist or a forest ranger. In secondary school, however, she discovered physics, the science that studies the laws which govern the world and seeks to understand what we are made of. She succeeded in combining her passion for the environment and her studies in physics to focus her research on nuclear techniques for the analysis of materials to study air pollution and climate change. Her work lets her travel to faraway places: from the mighty heat of Delhi, India, to the extreme cold of the Arctic.
Researchers at work, p. 12

SILVIA NAVA

Silvia Nava is a professor at the Department of Physics and Astronomy at the University of Florence as well as a researcher at the INFN. As a child, she wanted to be a farmer and an expert in pecorino cheese. She didn't even know physics existed! Then in secondary school she began studying the great philosophers, who posed many questions: what are we made of? How was the universe born? And she understood that physics could answer these questions. Today she analyses environmental samples collected at the North Pole and South Pole to study air pollution and climate change, and also examines ancient particles that have been trapped in the ice for thousands of years.
Researchers at work, p. 13

© 2021 Sassi Editore Srl
Viale Roma 122/b
36015 Schio (VI) - Italy

INFN coordination: Anna Dalla Vecchia, Mariaelena Fedi and Sabine Hemmer
Text: Gioia Alfonsi and Giulia Pesavento
Illustrations: Enrico Lorenzi
Layout: Alberto Borgo
Translation: SallyAnn DelVino